CATS AND KITTENS
GRACE POND

For millions, the beauty and grace of the cat are without equal in the animal world. Whatever your fancy you'll find your favourite cat portrayed here. For this ravishing collection of photographs—over half of them in full colour—covers all the main breeds and varieties: the Long-hairs, from the Whites and Tabbies to the exotic Chinchillas, Blue Persians and Birmans; the British Short-hairs, from household pets to the rare Creams and Silver Spotteds; the Foreign Short-hairs—whether Abyssinian, Havana, Burmese or Rex—and the wonderful range of Siamese with their different coloured 'points'.

Accompanying the photographs is a typically evocative and informative introduction by the doyen of cat-writers, Grace Pond. Mrs Pond, who is the Show Organizer of the annual National Cat Club Championship Show at Olympia, has been breeding, showing and judging cats for many years. She is also a Fellow of the Zoological Society.

28 Colour plates
20 Black and white illustrations
64 Pages

overleaf Striking orange-eyed Long-hair White

CATS AND KITTENS

Grace Pond

Photographs by
Anne Cumbers and others

B. T. Batsford Ltd
London

ISBN 7134 3247 0
© Grace Pond and B. T. Batsford Ltd 1976
First published 1976
Printed in Great Britain by Acolortone Ltd, Ipswich, Suffolk
for the publishers
B. T. Batsford Ltd, 4 Fitzhardinge Street, London W1H 0AH

Contents

Acknowledgments

The Author and Publishers wish to thank
the following for permission to reproduce the
illustrations appearing in this book:
C. A. Adriaanse for pages 62 and 63
Animal Photography for page 61
Bavaria Verlag for page 17
Camera Clix for pages 15, 29, 31, 36, 43 and 46
Anne Cumbers for the frontispiece and pages 2, 9 (both), 11,
13 (bottom), 15, 19, 21, 29, 30, 32, 33, 35, 37-41 42-44,
47, 50-55, 57 and 58-60.
J. Hunt for page 13 (top)
Lensart/Camera Press Ltd for page 19
Kenneth Scowen for pages 27 and 34
Tivey and Hattan for page 84

COVER ILLUSTRATIONS
Front: Tabby Kitten – Spectrum Colour Library
Back: Siamese at play – C. A. Adriaanse

Introduction

The cat, of all the animals in the world, is probably the best known and the most commonplace. The majority are mongrel short-coated cats with no known parentage, but even so they differ in appearance from country to country and island to island. In the East they are invariably long-bodied, with small heads, some with long tapering tails, others with kinked or even bent tails, while in Britain and other parts of Europe the heads tend to be rounder and the bodies and tails shorter (or, as in the Isle of Man, they have no tails at all). The colours and coat patterns vary greatly, usually conforming to no set standards, but it is from the ancestors of these cats in the not-so-distant past that the very decorative pedigree aristocrats seen in the cat world today were developed.

Some countries, such as Australia, originally had no resident domestic cats, but gradually, through sailors, travellers and the early settlers, they were spread

Blue Burmese female with her Brown Burmese kitten

A pair of demure Cream Long-hair kittens

Short-haired Tortoiseshell-and-White—a female only variety

throughout the world. It is generally accepted that they originated in Egypt, evolving there from the desert wild cats, which had become domesticated over the years through close proximity to civilisation. Knowing cats, I am sure they would readily appreciate the possibilities of easy feeding and the probable attentions given them by the children. They became much valued as guardians of the granaries, protecting the grain from the ravages of rodents, and were eventually worshipped in the shape of Pasht, the cat-headed goddess, one of the Egyptian deities.

Since those days they have suffered many vicissitudes, and were associated with the occult in the Middle Ages when they were thought to be companions of witches and familiars of the Devil. It was in Victorian times that they really came into their own once more, probably as mice-catchers and also for their companionship. No one had really thought of the possibility of breeding any particular cats until 1871 when a Mr Harrison Weir organised the first official cat show, which was held at the Crystal Palace. This proved to be the forerunner of all the cat shows held today and the start of the international Cat Fancy throughout the world.

Haphazard matings were tried at first with unexpected results and it was soon appreciated that, to produce certain colours and patterns to order, it was necessary to know something of the cats' background. Thus records of parentage began to be kept and pedigrees were started. At the early shows the majority of the exhibits had short fur, although there were a few cats with long coats from Turkey, known as Angoras, and from Persia, the Persians. They were usually referred to as 'Foreign' cats to differentiate them from the resident short-coated British cats. The Long-hairs proved to be more popular than the Short-hairs, and for a while the short-coated cats suffered a decline.

Visitors came from overseas and many kittens were exported to form the basic breeding stock for new cat fancies. As there was no quarantine in those days new cats were also brought into Britain, including the Siamese. When these were first seen, one paper reported that they were more like monkeys than cats. Soon, however, their very distinctive appearance, with pale cream body colouring, the dark brown points, their beautiful blue eyes, and above all their personality, made them ever increasingly popular. Today there are more Siamese bred than any other variety.

There are numerous legends about the origin of many of the varieties now being bred. Some were said to have come from the palaces of Eastern potentates, only being allowed out of the country when given as gifts to foreigners for services rendered. It is possible that there is some element of truth in these tales as an

unusual-looking kitten may well have been sent to the palace to be treasured and possibly bred from. It must be confessed that much is supposition and such varieties as the Abyssinians, the Russian Blues and later the Burmese seen today are the results of careful selective breeding. So successful have the breeding programmes been that it is now possible to have nine or more point colour variations in the Siamese, ten or more Burmese, and five or more in the Abyssinians.

There are now over seventy recognised varieties of pedigree cats, divided into two main breeds, the long-haired and the short-haired. The Short-hairs are again divided into two main categories: the British and the Foreign (which includes the Siamese and the Rex). Each variety has a standard of points for which one hundred points are allocated for the various characteristics required to make up what would be the perfect specimen if it was ever born. The Governing Council of the Cat Fancy, which is the registering body for cats in Britain, acting in the same capacity as the Kennel Club in the dog world, only recognise a standard when variety breeds true for at least three generations and enough people are interested in breeding them. Breeding true means that when like is mated to like the kittens resemble the parents.

In this short introduction it is not possible to give very full descriptions of the many pedigree varieties, but I give brief details for the guidance of those considering buying a pedigree kitten. There are many cat shows held all over Britain and if you are not sure of the kind you prefer you should ideally visit a local show and study the various exhibits and talk to the breeders about them. If you are considering breeding or showing, the kitten you choose should be near as possible to the recognised standard; but if you want a kitten as a pet, it will not matter in the slightest if the ears are too big for a long-hair, or if the head is too round for a Siamese.

LONG-HAIRS

Taking the Long-hairs first, the heads should, for most varieties, be broad and round, with good width between the small tufted ears. The cheeks should be round and full, the noses short and broad, and the eyes round and large, with colour in keeping with the variety. The bodies should be cobby on low sturdy legs, with the tails very full and short, with no kinks or defects. The coats are very important, and should be very full, soft and silky, not woolly to the touch, with the fur around the heads being long, so that when brushed up it forms a soft frame for the faces.

Chocolate Burmese male, with good profile

Birman kitten, showing distinctive white gloves

There are several self-colours in the Long-hairs, that is the coat is the same colour all over, right down to the roots. These include the Black, one of the original varieties recognised, but still comparatively rare. When adult, the fur is jet-black, but in the kitten stage may be rusty-brown, even with greyish or white hairs in the coat. As the kitten matures, so the fur becomes a dense black, making a beautiful contrast with the copper colour eyes. The black fur tends to react to strong sunlight and also to damp, so, if you are thinking of showing, it is as well to keep the cat away from the elements for a few weeks prior to the show.

Another self-coloured is the White, which is rapidly increasing in popularity. Three eye-colourings are possible: the Blue-eyed, with eyes of deep blue; the Orange-eyed, which may have eyes of deep orange of copper, and the Odd-eyed, with one of blue and one of orange. Deafness may affect some strains of those with blue eyes, but not all. It is difficult to tell in a young kitten if it is deaf, as they react so quickly to movement.

The Creams, another self-coloured, have fur the colour of Devonshire cream, even in colour, and eyes of deep copper colour. Some Creams tend to have a reddish line along their backs, which is known as 'hot' and is a fault when being shown.

The Blues have always been very popular, with fur the same even colour all over, but any shade of blue is permitted, with the lighter colour seeming to be preferred. The large round eyes may be deep orange or copper in colour. An outstanding Blue comes very close to all that is required in the recognised standard.

One of the rarest of the Long-hairs is the Red Self, with fur of deep rich red and eyes of deep copper. The long silky coat should be free of tabby markings, but it is very difficult to breed without any bars or markings, these usually appearing on the face. They may appear in litters with Red Tabbies.

There are three varieties of long-haired tabbies: the Brown, with background fur of rich tawny sable, and markings of jet black, and with eyes of hazel or copper colouring; the Red, with deep red coat and even deeper and richer red markings, and eyes of deep copper; and the Silver Tabby, with pure silver coat having definite jet black markings, and eyes of green or hazel. The pattern of tabby markings is the same whether on a long-hair or short-hair, but is much easier to see on the short fur. There should be a distinct 'M' mark on the forehead, with swirls on the cheeks, and pencillings around the eyes resembling spectacles. From above, the shoulder patterning should look like a large butterfly. Around the chest should be two unbroken lines, like necklaces, and along the spine two wide bars, while the tail should be ringed, and the front of the legs regularly striped.

The Chinchilla is a delightful variety, with the pure white fur being delicately tipped with black, the tippings being evenly distributed on the back, sides, head and tail, giving a sparkling silver appearance. The tip of the nose should be brick-red, the emerald or blue-green eyes being rimmed with black.

Another striking variety is the Smoke with undercoat of near-white, with the fur shading to black at the tips—so much so that when standing still the cat appears to have black fur and it is not until it is seen in motion that the striking silver contrast is seen. The head and face should be black attractively framed with a silver frill, while the eyes may be orange or copper in colour.

The Smoke is an old variety, but is still comparatively rare, and if a kitten is wanted it may have to be ordered from the breeder. It is also possible to have a Blue Smoke with blue replacing the black.

There are several female-only varieties, with any males being born invariably proving to be sterile. There is the Tortoiseshell with a beautiful patched coat of black, red and cream: the colours should be bright, with the patches quite distinct from one another, and the eyes may be deep orange or copper. Another is the much-admired Tortoiseshell and White, with the patches of black, red and cream interspersed with white. The eyes may be orange or copper. The Blue-Cream too is a female-only variety, with fur of the two colours softly intermingling, giving a shot-silk effect, and with eyes of copper or orange colour. It is a difficult variety to produce without cream or blue patches, but is easier to breed as a Blue or Cream male may be used as a stud, with the resultant litters possibly containing Cream, Blue and Blue-Cream kittens.

Another distinctive variety is the Bi-colour, with coat of any two solid colours, such as black and white, and red and white. The standard says that 'not more than two thirds of the fur to be of the colour and not more than half white, and the colours must be clear and well distributed'.

Produced some years ago by selective breeding, the Colourpoint, with the striking Siamese coat pattern, has typical long-hair type and beautiful large blue eyes. As with the Siamese it is possible to have different points colouring with the pale body:

Cream with seal points
Glacial white with blue points
Ivory with chocolate points
Magnolia with lilac points

Off-white with red points
Cream with tortie points.

The tails should be short and full and without kinks or defects.

There are two kinds of cats which differ from other long-hairs in that the fur is not so luxurious and the heads are not so round and broad. One is the Birman, with similar coat pattern to that of the Colourpoint, but with the attractive feature of white gloved paws; those on the back legs, ending in points like gauntlets. The fur should be more golden beige than cream; the tail bushy, but not short, and the eyes a bright china blue.

The other is the Turkish, which was introduced into this country direct from Turkey, and is said to have the same type as the first long-hairs ever seen. The short wedge-shaped head, the large upright ears, and long nose gives the cat a slightly foreign look. The body is long but sturdy and the tail of medium length. The fur is chalk white with auburn markings on the face, the tail being ringed with the same colour, and the eyes are light amber in colour, with pink-skinned rims.

It is also possible to breed other cats with long fur that do not conform to any specific standard. At the moment these may be registered as 'Any Other Colour'. Such cats are those with coats the colour of milk chocolate and also lilac, which will doubtless become new varieties in due course.

SHORT-HAIRS

The cats with short fur are divided into two main breeds, the British and the Foreign (which includes the Siamese). The characteristics for the British varieties are the same, that is the heads should be broad, with well-developed cheeks; the faces short, with shortish noses, and small slightly rounded ears; powerful bodies on sturdy legs; tails thick at the base, the length in proportion to the bodies, with the fur short fine and close. The colours recognised are very similar to the long-hairs: the Blacks with shining jet black fur, with no white hairs; the Whites with the three eye colourings; the Cream, which is difficult to produce without tabby markings, and without rings on the tails; the Blue-Cream with intermingled fur of the two colours; the Tortoiseshells and the Tortoiseshells and White; the Smoke with silver undercoat, and the three Tabbies, Brown Red and Silver. The British Blue is most favoured and is probably the most typical of the British cats, really square-looking, with a good broad head, and sturdy body. The big round

eyes are most expressive and add character to the face.

There are two British varieties with patterned coats not found in the Long-hairs. These are the Spotted, one of the oldest varieties known, but which practically died out for some years, but has comparatively recently appeared again. Many excellent examples may be seen at the shows with the spotting being quite distinct and most attractive to see. Any colour is allowed with the spotting to be in keeping with the ground colour, as for example, silver fur with black spots.

The other variety is the Mackerel-striped Tabby which should have markings as dense as possible, with rings running vertically from the spine towards the ground, and neatly ringed tails.

Included with the British cats is the one variety, the Manx, that differs from all others, being completely without a tail, and having an indentation where the tail should start. It is also possible to have a Stumpy, having only a stump of tail. Manx mated to Manx may produce cats with tails.

The Manx coats should be double, soft and open like a rabbit's, with a thick undercoat; their heads round and large, but not resembling long-hair types; the noses longish; the cheeks prominent; the ears wide at the base, and tapering slightly to a point. Any colour or coat pattern is allowed, but the cats must have high hind-quarters and short back, giving the typical rabbit gait, so characteristic of the Manx.

The Foreign Short-hairs differ greatly from the British cats in appearance and all should have long graceful bodies, long tails and narrow heads, but each variety differs slightly from the other.

The Russian Blue should have fur of clear blue, short, thick and silky like seal skin, with head a short wedge in shape and having a flat skull, with prominent whisker pads; the almond-shaped eyes a vivid green in colour, and the ears large and pointed, their skin being very thin, almost transparent; the body long and graceful, and the tail fairly long and tapering.

There are now several colour variations being bred in the Abyssinians. The original had ruddy brown fur, double or treble ticked with black or dark brown, and there are now the Reds with fur of rich copper red, ticked with darker bands of the colour; the Blues and the Cream, both with double or triple ticking in keeping with the body colour; other colours are possible and are being shown in the Any Other Colour Abyssinian classes at the shows. Whatever the colour, the general characteristics are the same: the heads medium-wedge with sharp, comparatively large ears; large expressive eyes, green, yellow or hazel in colour; slender bodies

and fairly long and tapering tails.

The Havanas are similar in build to the Siamese, with long, well-proportioned heads and large pricked ears; long lithe bodies on slim dainty legs, with the hind ones being slightly higher than the front legs, with the tails long and tapering; a striking feature is the decidedly green slanting oriental eyes. The short glossy fur is a rich chestnut brown. This is still a comparatively rare variety.

The Burmese were introduced into Britain from America in the late 1940s and for the first year or two, only a few were seen, but the numbers have now increased out of all knowledge, so much so that they tend to rival the Siamese. The original Burmese had coats a rich dark seal brown in colour with a very glossy sheen, with a slight impression of points, short and fine in texture, lying close to the body. It is now possible to have many colour variations, such as the very popular Blue, with fur a bluish-grey, being a little darker on the back, the faint points shading to silver grey; the whole coat having a silver sheen. There is also the Chocolate, with coat the colour of warm milk chocolate; the Lilac with fur a delicate pinkish dove-grey; the Red with coat a rich golden red, shading to a lighter colour on the

Burmese kittens—Brown, Blue, Chocolate, Lilac and Cream

chest and belly; the Tortie, with the coat a mixture of brown, cream and red, with no obvious barring. Other colours now being bred are the Creams, the Blue Creams, the Chocolate Torties, and the Lilac Torties, all produced by careful selected breeding and all requiring similar characteristics. The heads are wedge-shaped, but shorter than the Siamese, and should be slightly rounded at the tops, with a profile break at the top of the noses. The bodies are medium in size, very elegant, on long slightly tapering legs. The eye colour varies slightly from yellowish green to yellow, but with the Brown, the eyes should be chartreuse. Really green eyes are a fault.

Similar in build to the Siamese are two of the newest varieties: the Foreign Lilac, with fur a deep lavender shade all over, and the Foreign White, with pure white fur, silky, short and close lying. They have graceful bodies, long whip like tails, and long wedge-shaped heads, with large pricked ears. Other foreign varieties are the Oriental Short hairs now being produced in a number of colours.

Most unusual in appearance are the Rex, Cornish and Devon, first discovered in the West country over twenty years ago, one in Cornwall and later one in Devon.

At first, although similar in appearance, it was presumed they were the same variety, but in time it was realised that they were, in fact, two separate varieties. Both should have curly, wavy coats, the Cornish being short and plushy, with the Devon short and fine, growing close to the skin. The heads are medium-wedge in shape, with the Cornish having longish straight noses and the Devon noses having strongly marked stops. The bodies are slender, of medium length and quite muscular, and the tails long, fine and tapering. The colours are various, with the eyes in keeping.

A recent arrival in Britain is the Korat, with the slate-blue fur having a definite silver sheen. A medium-sized cat with an attractive heart-shaped face, small head, with large ears and brilliant green or amber eyes, the numbers seen as yet are comparatively rare.

SIAMESE

The most popular of the pedigree varieties is the Siamese, medium-sized cat, with long svelte bodies on slim legs; the hind legs being slightly higher than the front ones; the feet being dainty and oval; the tails long and tapering. The heads are long, with width between the oriental-shaped vivid blue eyes, and the ears large and pricked. The heads should be wedge-shaped, neither round nor pointed; the noses long and straight, with no break.

The varieties recognised are:

Seal-Pointed, with cream body colour and seal brown points.
Blue-Pointed, with glacial white body colour and blue points.
Chocolate-Pointed, with ivory body colour and milk chocolate points.
Lilac-Pointed, with off-white body colour and pinkish-grey points.
Tabby-Pointed, with pale body colour conforming to the colouring of the
    points. The stripes on the masks and legs to be clearly defined.
Red-Pointed, with white body colour and bright reddish gold points.
Tortie-Pointed, with pale body colouring conforming with the points, which
    should be patched or mingled with red and/or cream.
Cream-Pointed, with cream body colour and deeper cream points.

Other variations are also being bred and include the Chocolate Tortie points, Blue Tortie points, Lilac Tortie points, Tabby Tortie points, Blue-Cream points and several others, all of which are now registered as Any Other Colour or Any Other Dilution Siamese.

A CAT'S CHARACTER

The character of a cat depends a great deal on its upbringing and training as a kitten, but the personality does vary from breed to breed and variety to variety. The Long-hairs are usually of quieter disposition than the Foreign short-hairs, showing affection readily, intelligent and playful, often behaving like kittens even when old. Very dignified in appearance, they are quite happy to be the only cat in the household.

If you are considering buying a Long-hair, remember that daily brushing and combing is essential to keep them looking immaculate and to remove any loose hairs in the coat which can cause 'fur ball'. This happens when a felt-like mass from hair licked down accummulates in the stomach and can cause problems.

The British Short-hairs are renowned for their equable disposition, being friendly and gentle, but highly intelligent, making delightful pets. They do need some grooming, but their short fine fur rarely tangles and brushing, light combing and hard hand-stroking once or twice a week being sufficient to keep the coats looking glossy and immaculate.

The Foreign Short-hairs vary in character and disposition more than the Long-hairs and British Short-hairs.

The Russian Blues are quiet and placid, becoming very attached to their owners, but not over-demonstrative. They make excellent family pets.

The Abyssinians adore being noticed, are exceedingly friendly, but are rarely noisy cats. They are inclined to be restless when bored and love being played with.

The Havanas make playful, intelligent pets, liking to be the centre of attention, as the Foreign Lilacs and Whites.

The Burmese are very friendly, but full of self-confidence. They love company and being admired, but are not so demanding as are the Siamese. At the shows they will do their utmost to be noticed, frequently putting out a paw to attract the attention of passers-by.

The Rex are very much individuals, playful and affectionate. The Cornish Rex is of quieter disposition than the Devon, who can be quite demanding if they feel they need attention.

The rare Korat is also of quiet personality, but is friendly and affectionate.

The Siamese can be very demanding cats, exhibitionists, affectionate, but sometimes very noisy, especially when in season, craving attention but always making charming companions. Early training is essential to prevent them becoming curtain climbers and furniture scratchers.

Grooming is no problem at all for the Foreign Short-hairs, including the Siamese. The short fine-textured coats only require light brushing and very little combing. Hard hand-stroking will give the fur a natural sheen and help the circulation, while finishing off the coat by polishing with a chamois leather or piece of velvet will give an extra gloss. The Rex will need very little brushing or combing, hard hand-stroking seeming to keep their coats looking soft and shining.

GENERAL CARE

A kitten is a responsibility and, before taking one on, you should realise that it means daily feeding, house-training, grooming and making arrangements for its welfare during the holidays. The cost of feeding must be taken into account, and there may be one or two vets bills for neutering, if this is to be done. If fed correctly, looked after well and inoculated against Feline Enteritis, most cats live to an healthy old age.

It is most important before buying a kitten to ask if it has been inoculated and to ask for the vet's certificate for this. If not already done, arrangements should be made for this as soon as the kitten had has a few days to settle down. In the meantime, it should not be allowed to mix with other cats for fear of infection. Feline Infectious Enteritis is a killer disease, almost invariably proving fatal, with death occurring so quickly, sometimes only a matter of hours after the first symptoms, that poison rather than an illness is blamed.

The best age to have a new kitten is when it is about twelve weeks old as by that age it should be fully weaned, eating four small meals a day and should have been inoculated.

If undecided about the variety you want it is a good idea, as I have mentioned, to visit a show and see the different kinds. It is better to book a kitten rather than to take it home straight from the show and to collect it two or three weeks later. Even if inoculated against Feline Infectious Enteritis there are illnesses, such as cat 'flu, which may be picked up at a show.

The kitten chosen should be in first-class condition, lively, with glossy fur, bright-eyed with no dirt in the corners. Inside the ears should be clean with no ear mites, usually referred to as canker, and under the tail there should be no signs of messiness. The mouth and gums should be a healthy pink colour, and the breath sweet. The stomach should not be swollen, for this may be a sign of worms. There should be no fleas in the coat and the kitten should be sturdy without being overfat.

Kittens can be so captivating when young and it is so easy to fall for the first one seen, but it is important to buy one that is really strong and healthy, rather than to buy trouble in the shape of a fragile kitten that may be ill constantly. If you do not intend to go in for breeding or showing, you will not need to worry about the finer points. It is unfair, however, to buy one as a pet, telling the breeder that it is not to be used for breeding and showing, and then to do so. No breeder likes to see what is obviously a pet kitten appearing on the show bench under her prefix.

If the kitten is to be a pet and not bred from, the sex is not so important nowadays, as neutering is fairly simple. 'Spaying' a female is more serious than castrating a male, necessitating a small cut in the side, and some stitching under a general anaesthetic. The vet should be consulted about the best age to have any particular kitten neutered, as it does depend on development. The ages suggested are about three-and-a-half months for a male and four-and-a-half to five for a female.

Many owners are worried about having this done, feeling that it may alter the character of the kitten, making it lazy and fat. This should not happen, if it is given ample attention and has plenty of playthings. A neutered animal is more home-loving, not tending to stray. A male will not spray around, leaving the pungent tom cat smell, and a female will not be yelling her head off to attract the male cats. Some females, particularly the Siamese, can be very noisy when in season.

A pedigree kitten is usually registered by the breeder, particularly if it is of show standard, and when it has a new owner, it must be transferred and a small fee paid for this. This is most important if the kitten is to be exhibited.

When the kitten first arrives at the new home, all doors and windows should be closed, and it should be allowed to wander around getting used to the new surroundings. Young children should be discouraged from picking up young kittens, as their bones are so fragile that they may be injured just by hugging. The correct way to hold a kitten is to place one hand underneath the chest and the other under the hind quarters. It should never be lifted by the back of the neck as this can tear the muscles. A mother cat only does this when the kittens are very tiny.

The breeder should give the new owner a diet sheet which should be strictly adhered to for a few days at least until the kitten has settled down. The diet eventually may include raw and cooked meat, rabbit, chicken, some fish (but not too often), tinned cats foods, all mixed with a few cornflakes or brown bread. Milk may be given, but it is a food rather than a drink and may tend to make some kittens very loose, so should be given with care at first. It is most important that there is always fresh water down for drinking.

At twelve weeks the kitten should be already house-trained, accustomed to using to toilet tray. Kittens learn very quickly, some knowing what to do by instinct. Three-week-old kittens will go to a toilet tray, use it and scratch and cover the excreta without ever been shown, even by the mother. After feeding or awaking from sleep, the kitten should be taken to the tray or to the garden. The contents must be changed frequently, as all cats dislike using dirty trays. It is as well to stand the tray on paper so that the contents are not showered all around. Should the kitten dirty elsewhere, clean the spot thoroughly and sprinkle pepper there to discourage further use. It is no use smacking a kitten for this, as it will not be realised that it is a punishment and will think the owner is being cruel.

It is not necessary to buy an expensive cat bed or basket for the kitten to sleep in: a cardboard box is ideal. Lined with newspaper and a piece of blanket, put well away from draughts, it can be easily be replaced.

A kitten must be trained not to scratch the furniture when sharpening the claws. If allowed to go into the garden, a tree or shrub may be used for this, otherwise a scratching pad or post may be bought from a pet shop or one improvised by twining string around the kitchen table leg or nailing a piece of thick carpet to a small plank. Every time the kitten attempts to use the furniture, a loud 'no', a pointed finger and removal to the proper place should be sufficient for it soon to realise what is meant.

Kittens are not delicate and should never be over-pampered or kept in too heated an atmosphere, although Siamese, more than most cats, do appreciate warmth.

As the kitten grows, the number of meals may be cut down, until eventually the adult cat is having two large meals a day at regular times.

Grass, which is a natural emetic, helping the cat to bring up any fur swallowed, should always be provided. It can be grown in a pot, if there is no garden.

Whatever the variety, the general care is much the same: all cats need affection and attention. Given this, they become decorative and much-loved pets, giving in repayment years of constant companionship.

Blue Long-hair, a worthy Grand Champion

Tortie-and-White kitten, another female only variety

Sleeping in the sun: a Red Tabby

Black Long-hair kitten, still with baby coat

Little Red Long-hair kitten, still
with baby blue eyes

An attractive Blue Cream,
another female only variety

A little Brown Short-hair Tabby

A rare variety—the British Short-hair Cream

A completely tail-less Manx

British Blue, with outstanding characteristics

'Any other Variety'

A distinctive Abyssinian, said to resemble cats beloved by the Ancient Egyptians

The Havana, with long
well-porportioned head

A graceful Foreign White

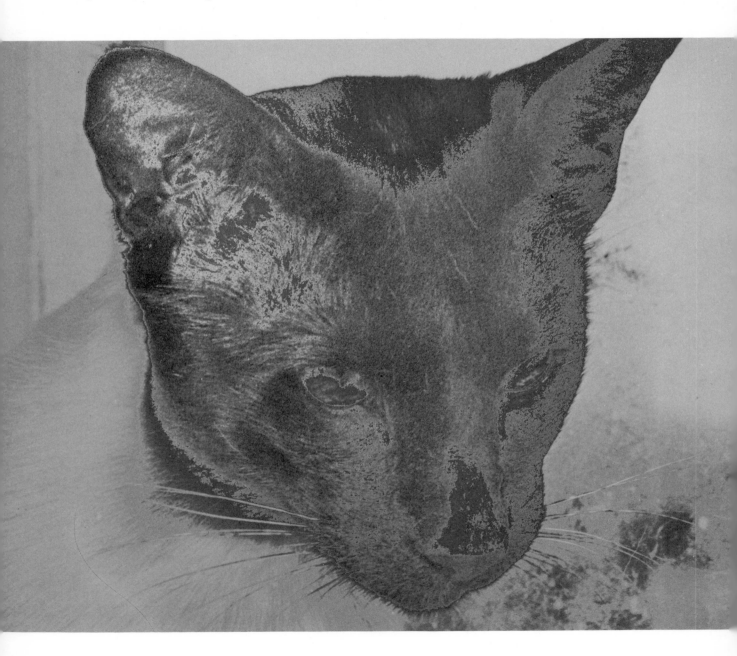

Tabby-point Siamese, with
wonderful eye shape